P9-CLH-638

150

Masterpieces of Drawing

Selected by Anthony Toney

Dover Publications, Inc., New York

Published in the United Kingdom by Constable and Company Limited, 10 Orange Street, London, W.C.2.

150 Masterpieces of Drawing is a new work, first published by Dover Publications, Inc., in 1963.

Library of Congress Catalog Card Number: 63-5656

Manufactured in the United States of America

Dover Publications, Inc., 180 Varick Street, New York 14, N.Y.

LIST OF PLATES

*All measurements are given in inches, with the width given before the height.

8 LEONARDO DA VINCI (Italian, 1452–1529).

Saint Peter. Silverpoint on blue tinted paper, continued with pen in bistre and lightly washed. Reproduced original size.

9 FRANCESCO BONSIGNORI (Italian, 1455–1519).

Portrait of a senator. Study for the signed painting in the National Gallery, London, dated 1487. Chalk (*Steinkreide*) on brown paper, with heightening in white. $10\frac{1}{4} \times 14$.

10 RAFFAELLINO DEL GARBO (Italian, 1466–1524).

Studies of hands for a Madonna and angels. Silverpoint on gray tinted paper. $9\frac{5}{8} \times 12\frac{1}{2}$.

11 BARTOLOMEO SUARDI, called BRAMMANTINO (Italian, ca. 1468–1535).

The Man of Sorrows. Pen drawing in bistre on brown paper, with wash and heightening in white. $6\frac{1}{16} \times 10\frac{1}{2}$.

12 MARCO D'OGGIONO (Italian, 1470–1530).

Madonna and Child. Formerly attributed to Leonardo da Vinci. Silverpoint on paper tinted blue and then varnished. $8\frac{1}{2} \times 10\frac{1}{4}$.

13 JAN GOSSAERT MABUSE (Flemish, ca. 1470–1541).

Adam and Eve seated on a root of the Tree of Knowledge. Pen drawing in bistre. $8\frac{1}{2} \times 10\frac{1}{4}$.

14 ALBRECHT DÜRER (German, 1471–1528).

Self portrait at the age of 13. Inscription: "*Dz hab Ich aws eim spigell nach mir selbs kunterfet im 1484 Jahr do ich noch ein Kint was* (This is the picture I did of myself looking into a mirror in 1484, when I was still a child)." Silverpoint on ivory-color tinted paper. $7\frac{3}{4} \times 10\frac{7}{8}$.

15 DÜRER.

Study for the "Saint Jerome" in Lisbon. Inscription: "*Der Man was alt 93 Jor vnd noch gesunt vnd fermuglich zv antorff* (This man was 93 years old and still healthy and active in Antwerp)." Signed and dated 1521. Brush drawing on gray violet tinted paper. $11\frac{1}{8} \times 16\frac{1}{2}$.

16 DÜRER.

Venetian woman in festive attire. Dated 1495. Lightly colored pen drawing. $6\frac{5}{8} \times 11\frac{1}{2}$.

17 DÜRER.

Portrait of Ulrich Varnbüler, of Nuremberg, Chief Counsel at the Supreme Court of the Holy Roman Empire. Preliminary drawing for the woodcut of 1522. Charcoal, the hair net in brown crayon. $12\frac{3}{4} \times 16\frac{1}{8}$.

18 DÜRER

The dead roller. (This is the bird known as *Blauracke* in Germany.) Dated 1512. Paints on parchment. $7\frac{7}{8} \times 10\frac{7}{8}$.

132 BOUCHER.
   Group of spectators. Brush drawing. $10\frac{3}{8} \times 15\frac{1}{2}$.

133 LOUIS AUBERT (French, 1720–1780).
   Two young artists in the studio; the seated boy is grinding colors. Black and red crayon and colored pencils. Dated 1747. $9\frac{1}{2} \times 13\frac{1}{8}$.

134 JEAN BAPTISTE GREUZE (French, 1725–1805).
   Maternal joy. Drawn with pen and brush over a pencil sketch, and colored with bistre. $11\frac{3}{4} \times 13\frac{1}{2}$.

135 GREUZE.
   Girl's head. Pastel on a reddish ground, enlivened with red crayon, and heightened with white. $10\frac{3}{16} \times 13\frac{1}{4}$.

136 GREUZE.
   Scene with a bound doe. Gray and brown wash. $14\frac{3}{8} \times 9\frac{1}{4}$.

137 JEAN HONORÉ FRAGONARD (French, 1732–1806).
   Fair of St. Cloud. Brush drawing with brown wash. $14\frac{7}{8} \times 9\frac{5}{8}$.

138 FRAGONARD.
   Bull and dog in stable. Brush drawing in bistre. $17\frac{1}{8} \times 12\frac{5}{8}$.

139 FRAGONARD.
   Expulsion of the merchants from the Temple. Pen drawing with brown wash. $18\frac{1}{16} \times 12\frac{3}{4}$.

140 FRAGONARD.
   Lion. Wash. $18 \times 13\frac{1}{8}$.

141 FRAGONARD.
   Girl with a marmot, probably Marguerite Gérard, the artist's sister-in-law. Brush drawing in bistre, with blue and red water color. $8\frac{3}{8} \times 10\frac{1}{4}$.

142 FRAGONARD.
   The great cypress avenue in the gardens of the Villa d'Este. Bistre. $13\frac{1}{4} \times 18$.

143 FRAGONARD.
   The vendor. Pencil sketch and brush drawing in bistre. $6\frac{3}{4} \times 9\frac{1}{4}$.

144 FRAGONARD.
   Children's merriment. Pencil sketch and execution in bistre. $6\frac{7}{8} \times 9\frac{3}{8}$.

145 FRAGONARD.
   Girl at a lectern (Marguerite Gérard). Brush drawing in bistre. $13\frac{5}{16} \times 17\frac{9}{16}$.

150

Masterpieces of Drawing

Plate 1. *Vittore Pisano, called Pisanello*

Plate 2. *Petrus Christus*

Plate 3. *Unknown Flemish master of the 15th century*

Plate 4. *Master of the Hausbuch*

Plate 5. *Pietro Perugino*

Plate 6. *Domenico Ghirlandaio*

Plate 7. *Francesco Francia*

Plate 8. *Leonardo da Vinci*

Plate 9. *Francesco Bonsignori*

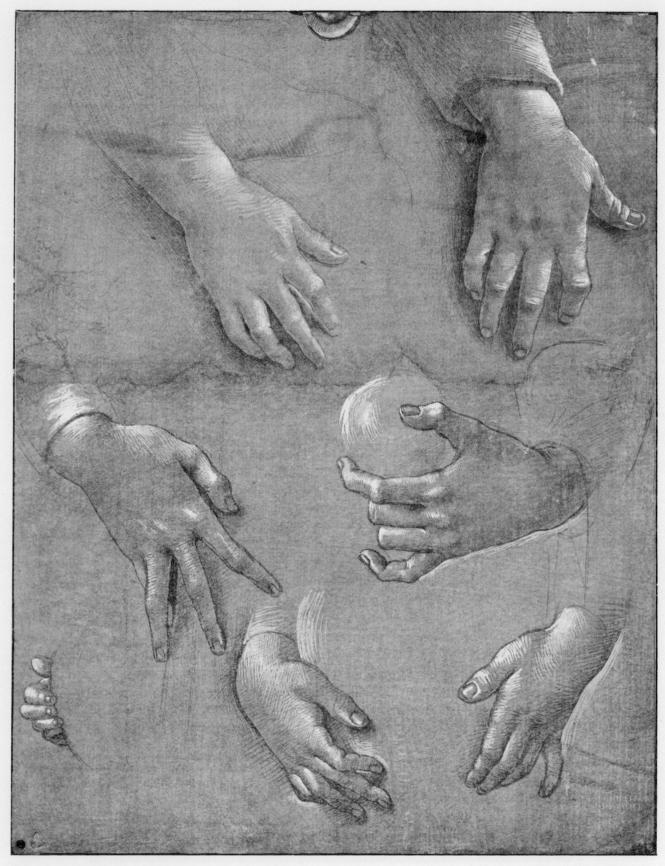

Plate 10. *Raffaellino del Garbo*

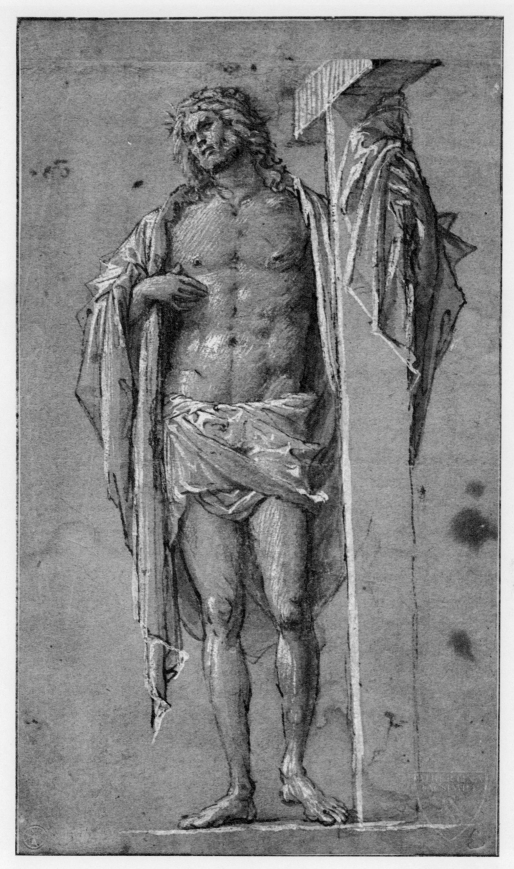

Plate 11. *Bartolommeo Suardi, called Bramantino*

Plate 12. *Marco d'Oggiono*

Plate 13. *Jan Gossaert Mabuse*

Plate 14. *Albrecht Dürer*

Plate 15. *Dürer*

Plate 16. *Dürer*

Plate 17. *Dürer*

Plate 18. *Dürer*

Plate 19. *Dürer*

Plate 20. *Dürer*

Plate 21. *Dürer*

Plate 22. *Dürer*

Plate 23. *Dürer*

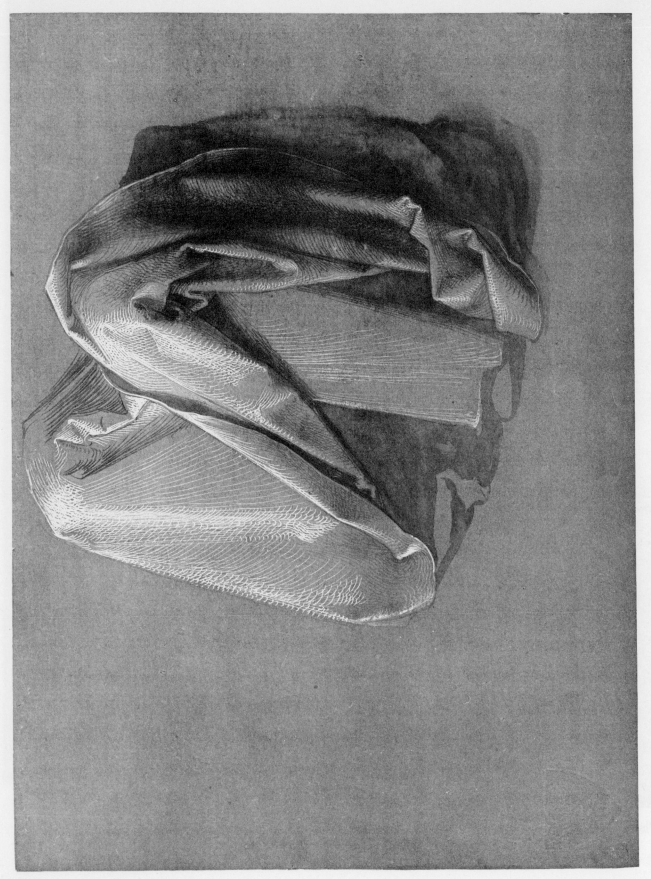

Plate 24. *Dürer*

Plate 25. *Dürer*

Plate 26. *Lukas Cranach the Elder*

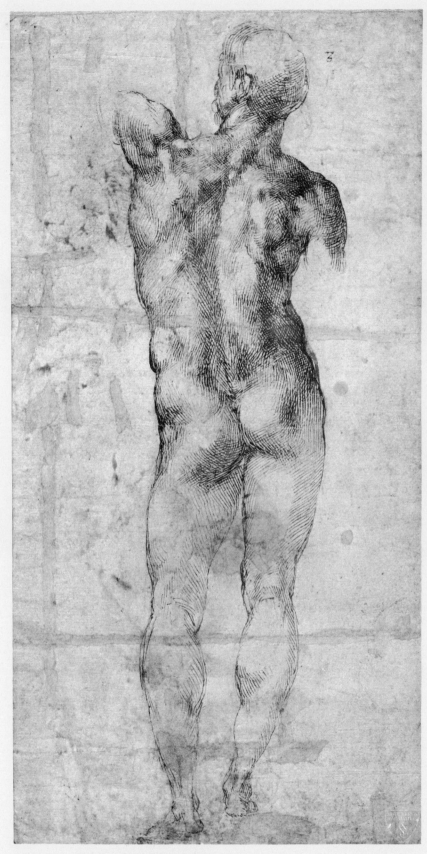

Plate 27. *Michelangelo Buonarroti*

Plate 28. *Michelangelo*

Plate 29. *Michelangelo*

Plate 30. *Bernardino Luini*

Plate 31. *Wolf Huber*

Plate 32. *Jörg Breu the Elder*

Plate 33. *Albrecht Altdorfer*

Plate 34. *Hans Baldung, called Grien*

Plate 35. *Baldung*

Plate 36. *Raffaele Santi* (Raphael)

Plate 37. *Raphael*

Plate 38. *Raphael*

Plate 39. *Raphael*

Plate 40. *Urs Graf*

Plate 41. *Marco Basaiti*

Plate 42. *François Clouet*

Plate 43. *Pieter Bruegel the Elder*

Plate 44. *Bruegel*

Plate 45. *Bruegel*

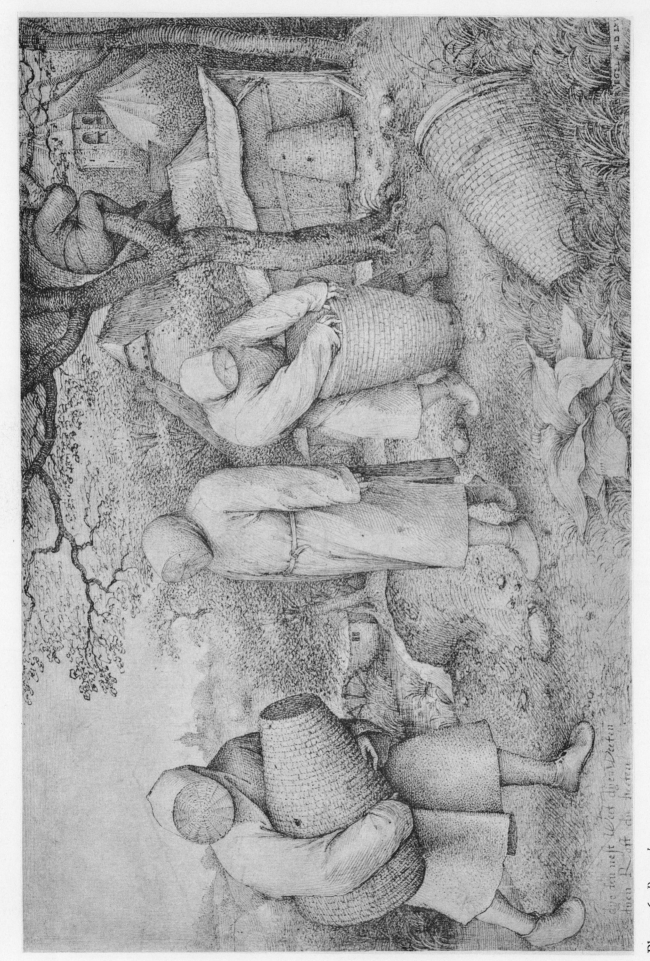

Plate 46. *Bruegel*

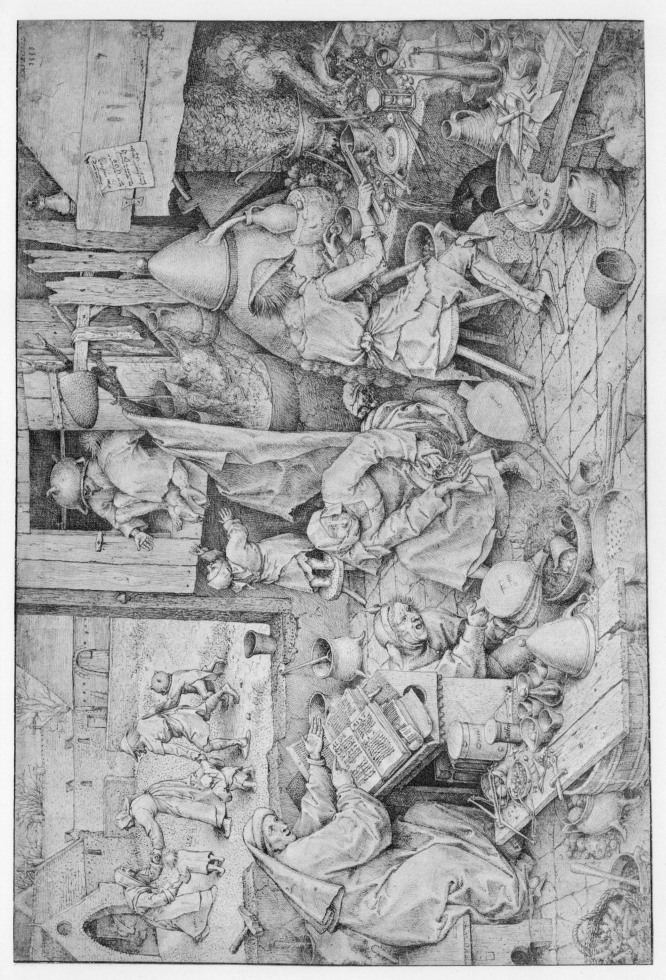

Plate 47. *Bruegel*

Plate 48. *Bruegel*

Plate 49. *Bruegel*

Plate 50. *Bruegel*

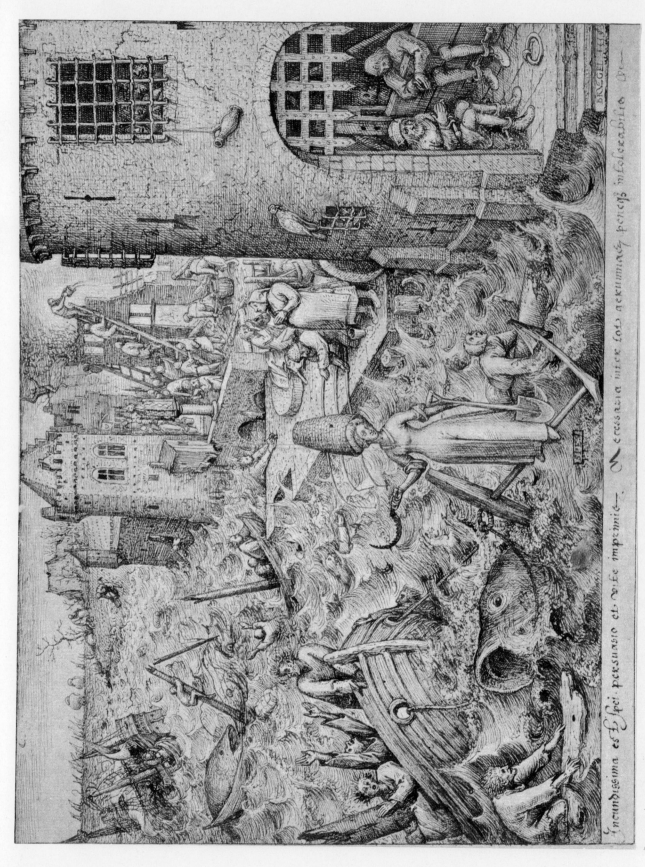

Plate 51. *Bruegel*

Plate 52. *Bruegel*

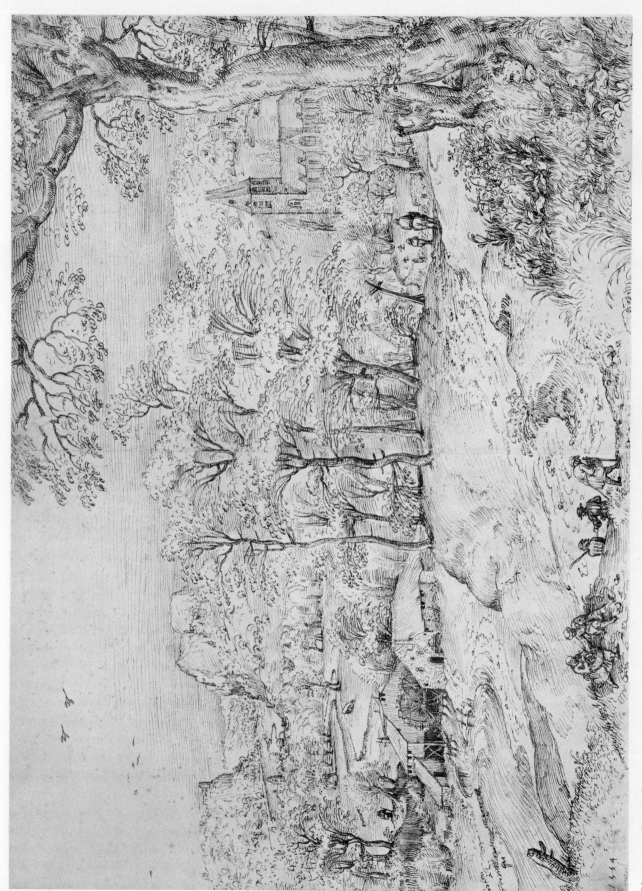

Plate 53. *Bruegel*

Plate 54. *Bruegel*

Plate 55. *Peter Paul Rubens*

Plate 56. *Rubens*

Plate 57. *Rubens*

Plate 58. *Rubens*

Plate 59. *Rubens*

Plate 60. *Rubens*

Plate 61. *Rubens*

Plate 62. *Rubens*

Plate 63. *Rubens*

Plate 64. *Rubens*

Plate 65. *Rubens*

Plate 66. *Rubens*

Plate 67. *Rubens*

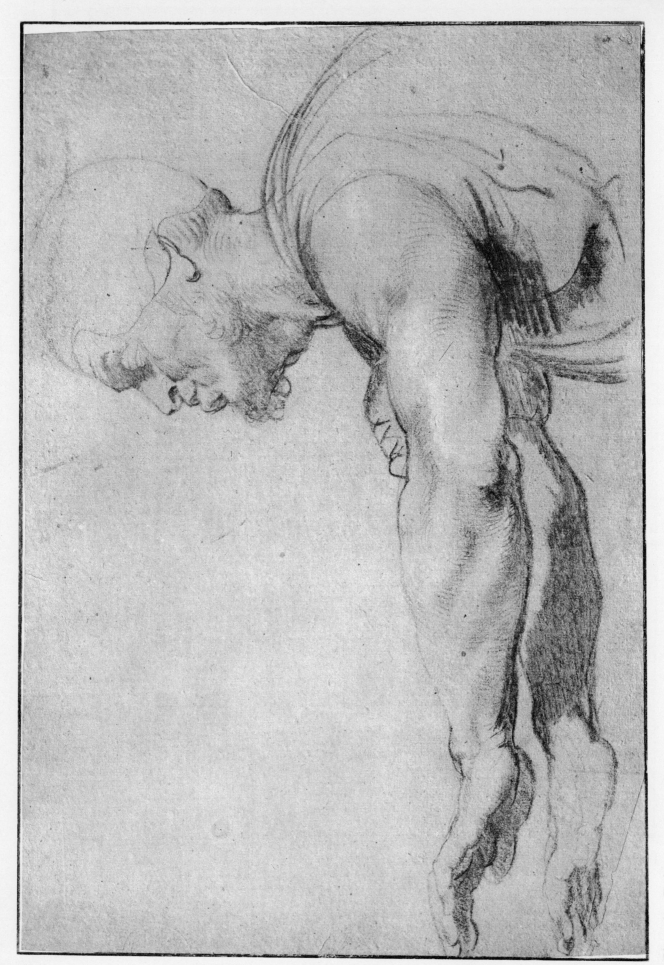

Plate 68. *Rubens*

Plate 69. *Rubens*

Plate 70. *Jacques Callot*

Plate 71. *Nicolas Poussin*

Plate 72. *Ian van Goyen*

Plate 73. *Anthonis van Dyck*

Plate 74. *Van Dyck*

Plate 75. *Van Dyck*

Plate 76. *Van Dyck*

Plate 77. *Salomon van Ruisdael*

Plate 78. *Adriaen Brouwer*

Plate 79. *Rembrandt Harmensz van Rijn*

Plate 80. *Rembrandt*

Plate 81. *Rembrandt*

Plate 82. *Rembrandt*

Plate 83. *Rembrandt*

Plate 84. *Rembrandt*

Plate 85. *Rembrandt*

Plate 86. *Rembrandt*

Plate 87. *Rembrandt*

Plate 88. *Rembrandt*

Plate 89. *Rembrandt*

Plate 90. *Rembrandt*

Plate 91. *Rembrandt*

Plate 92. *Rembrandt*

Plate 93. *Rembrandt*

Plate 94. *Rembrandt*

Plate 95. *Rembrandt*

Plate 96. *Rembrandt*

Plate 97. *Rembrandt*

Plate 98. *Rembrandt*

Plate 99. *Rembrandt*

Plate 100. *Rembrandt*

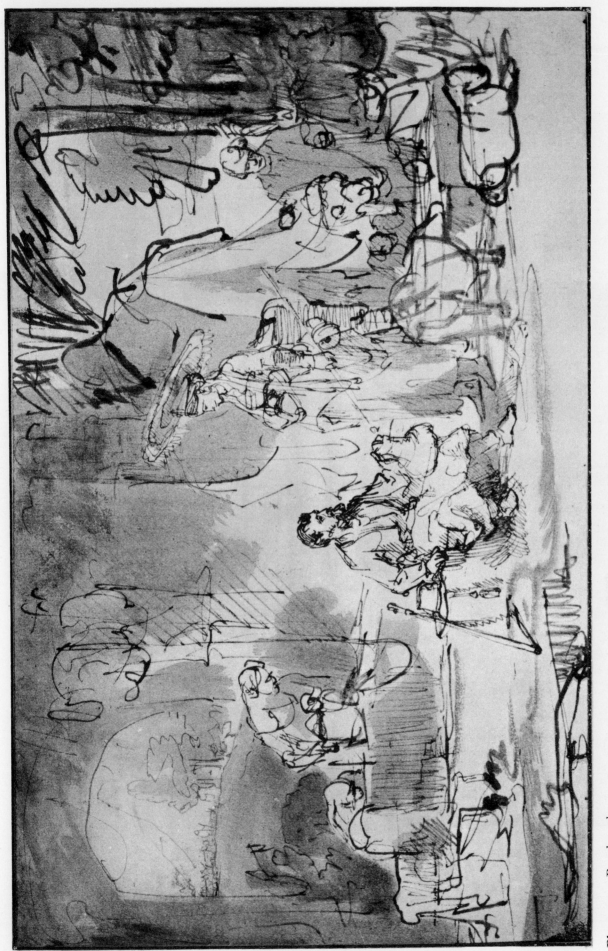

Plate 101. *Rembrandt*

Plate 102. *Rembrandt*

Plate 103. *Rembrandt*

Plate 104. *Rembrandt*

Plate 105. *Rembrandt*

Plate 106. *David Teniers the Younger*

Plate 107. *Bartholomeus van der Helst*

Plate 108. *Ferdinand Bol*

Plate 109. *Sir Peter Lely*

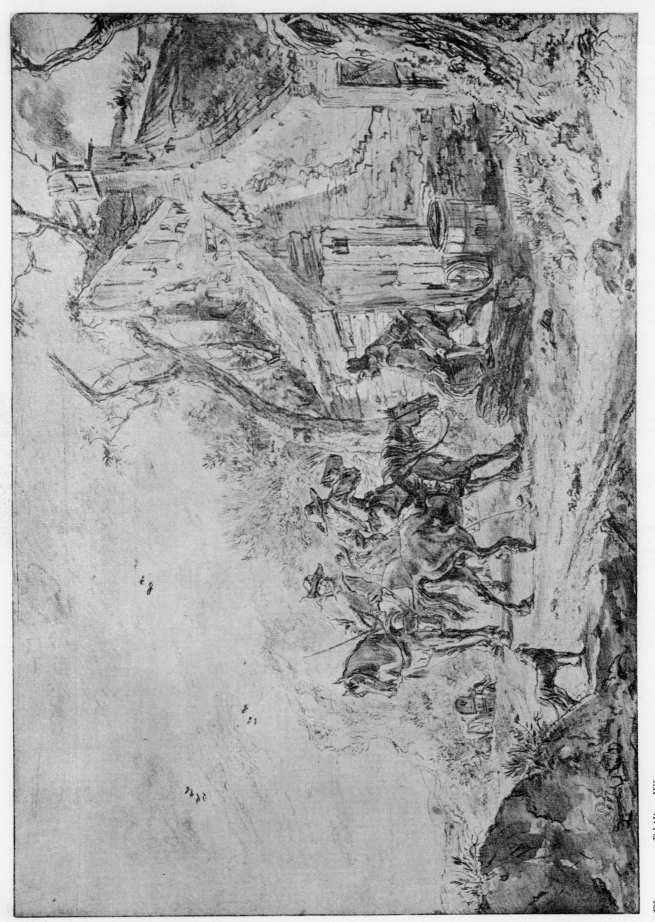

Plate 110. *Philips Wouverman*

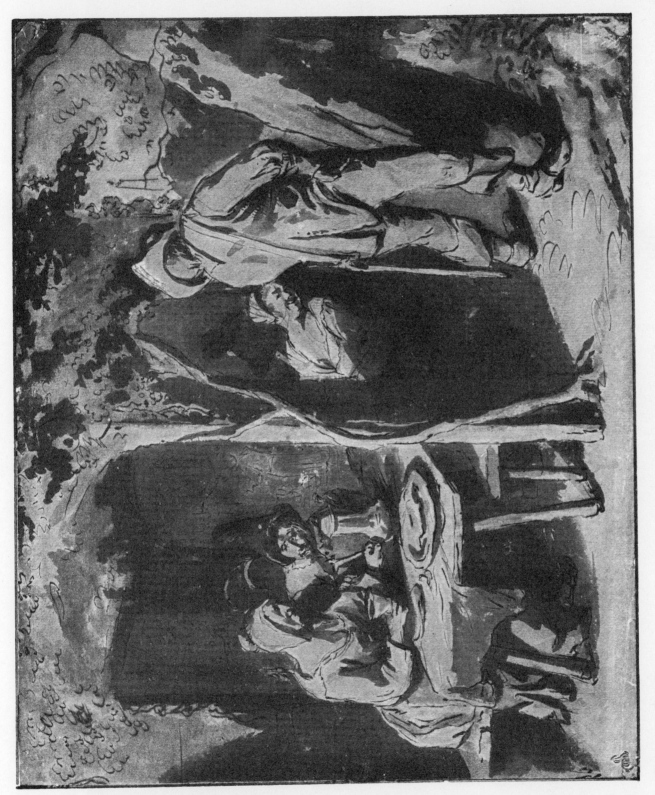

Plate 111. *Jan Steen*

Plate 112. *Jacob van Ruisdael*

Plate 113. *Jan Vermeer van Delft*

Plate 114. *Antoine Watteau*

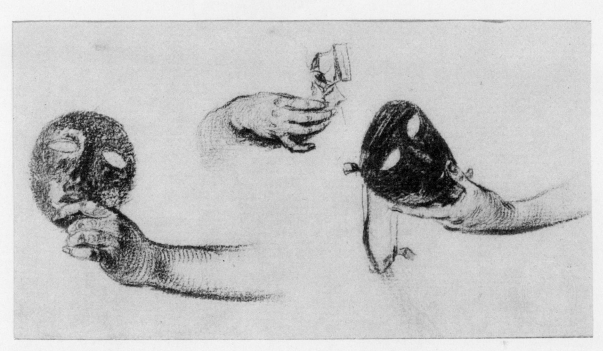

Plate 115. *Watteau*

Plate 116. *Watteau*

Plate 117. *Watteau*

Plate 118. *Watteau*

Plate 119. *Antoine Pesne*

Plate 120. *Nicolas Lancret*

Plate 121. *Lancret*

Plate 122. *Giovanni Battista Tiepolo*

Plate 123. *Antonio Canale, called Canaletto*

Plate 124. *Jean-Baptiste Siméon Chardin*

Plate 125. *Chardin*

Plate 126. *Charles-Joseph Natoire*

Plate 127. *Jean Etienne Liotard*

Plate 128. *François Boucher*

Plate 129. *Boucher*

Plate 130. *Boucher*

Plate 131. *Boucher*

Plate 132. *Boucher*

Plate 133. *Louis Aubert*

Plate 134. *Jean Baptiste Greuze*

Plate 135. *Greuze*

Plate 136. *Greuze*

Plate 137. *Jean Honoré Fragonard*

Plate 138. *Fragonard*

Plate 139. *Fragonard*

Plate 140. *Fragonard*

Plate 141. *Fragonard*

Plate 142. *Fragonard*

Plate 143. *Fragonard*

Plate 144. *Fragonard*

Plate 145. *Fragonard*

Plate 146. *Fragonard*

Plate 147. *Fragonard*

Plate 148. *Hubert Robert*

Plate 149. *Augustin de Saint-Aubin*

Plate 150. *Saint-Aubin*

Dover Books on Art

VASARI ON TECHNIQUE, G. Vasari. Pupil of Michelangelo, outstanding biographer of Renaissance artists reveals technical methods of his day. Marble, bronze, fresco painting, mosaics, engraving, stained glass, rustic ware, etc. Only English translation, extensively annotated by G. Baldwin Brown. 18 plates. 342pp. 5⅜ x 8.   **T717 Paperbound $2.00**

FOOT-HIGH LETTERS: A GUIDE TO LETTERING, M. Price. 28 16″ x 22″ plates, give classic Roman alphabet, one foot high per letter, plus 9 other 2″-high letter forms for each letter. 16 page syllabus. Ideal for lettering classes, home study. 28 plates in box.   **T239 $6.00**

A HANDBOOK OF WEAVES, G. H. Oelsner. Most complete book of weaves, fully explained, differentiated, illustrated. Plain weaves, irregular, double-stitched, filling satins; derivative, basket, rib weaves; steep, broken, herringbone, twills, lace, tricot, many others. Translated, revised by S. S. Dale; supplement on analysis of weaves. Bible for all handweavers. 1875 illustrations. 410pp. 6⅛ x 9¼.   **T209 Clothbound $5.00**

JAPANESE HOMES AND THEIR SURROUNDINGS, E. S. Morse. Classic describes, analyses, illustrates all aspects of traditional Japanese home, from plan and structure to appointments, furniture, etc. Published in 1886, before Japanese architecture was contaminated by Western, this is strikingly modern in beautiful, functional approach to living. Indispensable to every architect, interior decorator, designer. 307 illustrations. Glossary. 408pp. 5⅝ x 8⅜.   **T746 Paperbound $2.00**

DESIGN FOR ARTISTS AND CRAFTSMEN, L. Wolchonok. The most thorough course on the creation of art motifs and designs. Shows you step-by-step, with hundreds of examples and 113 detailed exercises, how to create original designs from geometric patterns, plants, birds, animals, humans, and man-made objects. "A great contribution to the field of design and crafts," N. Y. SOCIETY OF CRAFTSMEN. More than 1300 entirely new illustrations. xv + 207pp. 7⅞ x 10¾.   **T274 Clothbound $4.95**

HANDBOOK OF DESIGNS AND DEVICES, C. P. Hornung. A remarkable working collection of 1836 basic designs and variations, all copyright-free. Variations of circle, line, cross, diamond, swastika, star, scroll, shield, many more. Notes on symbolism. "A necessity to every designer who would be original without having to labor heavily," ARTIST AND ADVERTISER. 204 plates. 240pp. 5⅜ x 8.   **T125 Paperbound $1.90**

THE UNIVERSAL PENMAN, George Bickham. Exact reproduction of beautiful 18th-century book of handwriting. 22 complete alphabets in finest English roundhand, other scripts, over 2000 elaborate flourishes, 122 calligraphic illustrations, etc. Material is copyright-free. "An essential part of any art library, and a book of permanent value," AMERICAN ARTIST. 212 plates. 224pp. 9 x 13¾.   **T20 Clothbound $10.00**

A DIDEROT PICTORIAL ENCYCLOPEDIA OF TRADES AND INDUSTRY. Manufacturing and the Technical Arts in Plates Selected from "L'Encyclopédie ou Dictionnaire Raisonné des Sciences, des Arts, et des Métiers," of Denis Diderot, edited with text by C. Gillispie. Over 2000 illustrations on 485 full-page plates. Magnificent 18th-century engravings of men, women, and children working at such trades as milling flour, cheesemaking, charcoal burning, mining, silverplating, shoeing horses, making fine glass, printing, hundreds more, showing details of machinery, different steps in sequence, etc. A remarkable art work, but also the largest collection of working figures in print, copyright-free, for art directors, designers, etc. Two vols. 920pp. 9 x 12. Heavy library cloth. T421 Two volume set $18.50

SILK SCREEN TECHNIQUES, J. Biegeleisen, M. Cohn. A practical step-by-step home course in one of the most versatile, least expensive graphic arts processes. How to build an inexpensive silk screen, prepare stencils, print, achieve special textures, use color, etc. Every step explained, diagrammed. 149 illustrations, 201pp. 6⅛ x 9¼. T433 Paperbound $1.55

STICKS AND STONES, Lewis Mumford. An examination of forces influencing American architecture: the medieval tradition in early New England, the classical influence in Jefferson's time, the Brown Decades, the imperial facade, the machine age, etc. "A truly remarkable book," SAT. REV. OF LITERATURE. 2nd revised edition. 21 illus. xvii + 240pp. 5⅜ x 8. T202 Paperbound $1.60

THE AUTOBIOGRAPHY OF AN IDEA, Louis Sullivan. The architect whom Frank Lloyd Wright called "the master" records the development of the theories that revolutionized America's skyline. 34 full-page plates of Sullivan's finest work. New introduction by R. M. Line. xiv + 335pp. 5⅜ x 8. T281 Paperbound $2.00

THE MATERIALS AND TECHNIQUES OF MEDIEVAL PAINTING, D. V. Thompson. An invaluable study of carriers and grounds, binding media, pigments, metals used in painting, al fresco and al secco techniques, burnishing, etc. used by the medieval masters. Preface by Bernard Berenson. 239pp. 5⅜ x 8. T327 Paperbound $1.85

ART ANATOMY, Dr. William Rimmer. One of the few books on art anatomy that are themselves works of art, this is a faithful reproduction (rearranged for handy use) of the extremely rare masterpiece of the famous 19th century anatomist, sculptor, and art teacher. Beautiful, clear line drawings show every part of the body—bony structure, muscles, features, etc. Unusual are the sections on falling bodies, foreshortenings, muscles in tension, grotesque personalities, and Rimmer's remarkable interpretation of emotions and personalities as expressed by facial features. It will supplement every other book on art anatomy you are likely to have. Reproduced clearer than the lithographic original (which sells for $500 on up on the rare book market.) Over 1,200 illustrations. xiii + 153pp. 7¾ x 10¾. T908 Paperbound $2.00

THE CRAFTSMAN'S HANDBOOK, Cennino Cennini. The finest English translation of IL LIBRO DELL' ARTE, the 15th century introduction to art technique that is both a mirror of Quattrocento life and a source of many useful but nearly forgotten facets of the painter's art. 4 illustrations. xxvii + 142pp. D. V. Thompson, translator. 5⅜ x 8.   T54 Paperbound $1.25

THE BROWN DECADES, Lewis Mumford. A picture of the "buried renaissance" of the post-Civil War period, and the founding of modern architecture (Sullivan, Richardson, Root, Roebling), landscape development (Marsh, Olmstead, Eliot), and the graphic arts (Homer, Eakins, Ryder). 2nd revised, enlarged edition. Bibliography. 12 illustrations. xiv + 266 pp. 5⅜ x 8.
     T200 Paperbound $1.65

THE HUMAN FIGURE, J. H. Vanderpoel. Not just a picture book, but a complete course by a famous figure artist. Extensive text, illustrated by 430 pencil and charcoal drawings of both male and female anatomy. 2nd enlarged edition. Foreword. 430 illus. 143pp. 6⅛ x 9¼.   T432 Paperbound $1.50

PINE FURNITURE OF EARLY NEW ENGLAND, R. H. Kettell. Over 400 illustrations, over 50 working drawings of early New England chairs, benches, beds, cupboards, mirrors, shelves, tables, other furniture esteemed for simple beauty and character. "Rich store of illustrations . . . emphasizes the individuality and varied design," ANTIQUES. 413 illustrations, 55 working drawings. 475pp. 8 x 10¾.   T145 Clothbound $10.00

BASIC BOOKBINDING, A. W. Lewis. Enables both beginners and experts to rebind old books or bind paperbacks in hard covers. Treats materials, tools; gives step-by-step instruction in how to collate a book, sew it, back it, make boards, etc. 261 illus. Appendices. 155pp. 5⅜ x 8.   T169 Paperbound $1.35

DESIGN MOTIFS OF ANCIENT MEXICO, J. Enciso. Nearly 90% of these 766 superb designs from Aztec, Olmec, Totonac, Maya, and Toltec origins are unobtainable elsewhere. Contains plumed serpents, wind gods, animals, demons, dancers, monsters, etc. Excellent applied design source. Originally $17.50. 766 illustrations, thousands of motifs. 192pp. 6⅛ x 9¼.
     T84 Paperbound $1.85

HAWTHORNE ON PAINTING. Vivid re-creation, from students' notes, of instructions by Charles Hawthorne at Cape Cod School of Art. Essays, epigrammatic comments on color, form, seeing, techniques, etc. "Excellent," TIME. 91pp. 5⅜ x 8.
     T653 Paperbound $1.00

BYZANTINE ART AND ARCHAEOLOGY, O. M. Dalton. Still most thorough work in English on Byzantine art forms throughout ancient and medieval world. Analyzes hundreds of pieces, covers sculpture, painting, mosaic, jewelry, textiles, bronze, glass, etc. Historical development; specific examples; iconology and ideas; symbolism. A treasure-trove of material about one of most important art traditions, will supplement and expand any other book in area. Bibliography of over 2500 items. 457 illustrations. 747pp. 6⅛ x 9¼.   T776 Clothbound $7.50

ANIMALS IN MOTION, Eadweard Muybridge. The largest collection of animal action photos in print. 34 different animals (horses, mules, oxen, goats, camels, pigs, cats, lions, gnus, deer, monkeys, eagles—and 22 others) in 132 characteristic actions. All 3919 photographs are taken in series at speeds up to 1/1600th of a second, offering artists, biologists, cartoonists a remarkable opportunity to see exactly how an ostrich's head bobs when running, how a lion puts his foot down, how an elephant's knee bends, how a bird flaps his wings, thousands of other hard-to-catch details. "A really marvellous series of plates," NATURE. 380 full-page plates. Heavy glossy stock, reinforced binding with headbands. 7⅞ x 10¾.　　　　　　　T203 Clothbound $10.00

THE HUMAN FIGURE IN MOTION, Eadweard Muybridge. The largest collection in print of Muybridge's famous high-speed action photos. 4789 photographs in more than 500 action-strip-sequences (at shutter speeds up to 1/6000th of a second) illustrate men, women, children—mostly undraped—performing such actions as walking, running, getting up, lying down, carrying objects, throwing, etc. "An unparalleled dictionary of action for all artists," AMERICAN ARTIST. 390 full-page plates, with 4789 photographs. Heavy glossy stock, reinforced binding with headbands. 7⅞ x 10¾.　　　　　　　T204 Clothbound $10.00

THE BOOK OF SIGNS, R. Koch. 493 symbols—crosses, monograms, astrological, biological symbols, runes, etc.—from ancient manuscripts, cathedrals, coins, catacombs, pottery. May be reproduced permission-free. 493 illustrations by Fritz Kredel. 104pp. 6⅛ x 9¼.　　　　　　　T162 Paperbound $1.00

A HANDBOOK OF EARLY ADVERTISING ART, C. P. Hornung. The largest collection of copyright-free early advertising art ever compiled. Vol. I: 2,000 illustrations of animals, old automobiles, buildings, allegorical figures, fire engines, Indians, ships, trains, more than 33 other categories! Vol. II: Over 4,000 typographical specimens; 600 Roman, Gothic, Barnum, Old English faces; 630 ornamental type faces; hundreds of scrolls, initials, flourishes, etc. "A remarkable collection," PRINTERS' INK.

Vol. I: Pictorial Volume. Over 2000 illustrations. 256pp. 9 x 12.
　　　　　　　T122 Clothbound $10.00

Vol. II: Typographical Volume. Over 4000 specimens. 319pp.
9 x 12.　　　　　　　T123 Clothbound $10.00

　　　　Two volume set, Clothbound, only $18.50

PRIMITIVE ART, Franz Boas. A great American anthropologist covers theory, technical virtuosity, styles, symbolism, patterns, etc. of primitive art. The more than 900 illustrations will interest artists, designers, craftworkers. Over 900 illustrations. 376pp. 5⅜ x 8.　　　　　　　T25 Paperbound $1.95

ON THE LAWS OF JAPANESE PAINTING, H. Bowie. The best possible substitute for lessons from an Oriental master. Treats both spirit and technique; exercises for control of the brush; inks, brushes, colors; use of dots, lines to express whole moods, etc. 66 illus. 272 pp. 6⅛ x 9¼.　　T30 Paperbound $1.95

AN ATLAS OF ANATOMY FOR ARTISTS, F. Schider. This standard work contains 189 full-page plates, more than 647 illustrations of all aspects of the human skeleton, musculature, cutaway portions of the body, each part of the anatomy, hand forms, eyelids, breasts, location of muscles under the flesh, etc. 59 plates illustrate how Michelangelo, da Vinci, Goya, 15 others, drew human anatomy. New 3rd edition enlarged by 52 new illustrations by Cloquet, Barcsay. "The standard reference tool," AMERICAN LIBRARY ASSOCIATION. "Excellent," AMERICAN ARTIST. 189 plates, 647 illustrations. xxvi + 192pp. 7⅞ x 10⅝. T241 Clothbound $6.00

AN ATLAS OF ANIMAL ANATOMY FOR ARTISTS, W. Ellenberger, H. Baum, H. Dittrich. The largest, richest animal anatomy for artists in English. Form, musculature, tendons, bone structure, expression, detailed cross sections of head, other features, of the horse, lion, dog, cat, deer, seal, kangaroo, cow, bull, goat, monkey, hare, many other animals. "Highly recommended," DESIGN. Second, revised, enlarged edition with new plates from Cuvier, Stubbs, etc. 288 illustrations. 153pp. 11⅜ x 9.
T82 Clothbound $6.00

ANIMAL DRAWING: ANATOMY AND ACTION FOR ARTISTS, C. R. Knight. 158 studies, with full accompanying text, of such animals as the gorilla, bear, bison, dromedary, camel, vulture, pelican, iguana, shark, etc., by one of the greatest modern masters of animal drawing. Innumerable tips on how to get life expression into your work. "An excellent reference work," SAN FRANCISCO CHRONICLE. 158 illustrations. 156pp. 10½ x 8½. T426 Paperbound $2.00

THE HISTORY AND TECHNIQUE OF LETTERING, A. Nesbitt. A thorough history of lettering from the ancient Egyptians to the present, and a 65-page course in lettering for artists. Every major development in lettering history is illustrated by a complete alphabet. Fully analyzes such masters as Caslon, Koch, Garamond, Jenson, and many more. 89 alphabets, 165 other specimens. 317pp. 7½ x 10½. T427 Paperbound $2.00

LETTERING AND ALPHABETS, J. A. Cavanagh. An unabridged reissue of "Lettering," containing the full discussion, analysis, illustration of 89 basic hand lettering styles based on Caslon, Bodoni, Gothic, many other types. Hundreds of technical hints on construction, strokes, pens, brushes, etc. 89 alphabets, 72 lettered specimens, which may be reproduced permission-free. 121pp. 9¾ x 8. T53 Paperbound $1.25

PRINCIPLES OF ART HISTORY, H. Wölfflin. This remarkably instructive work demonstrates the tremendous change in artistic conception from the 14th to the 18th centuries, by analyzing 164 works by Botticelli, Dürer, Hobbema, Holbein, Hals, Titian, Rembrandt, Vermeer, etc., and pointing out exactly what is meant by "baroque," "classic," "primitive," "picturesque," and other basic terms of art history and criticism. "A remarkable lesson in the art of seeing," SAT. REV. OF LITERATURE. Translated from the 7th German edition. 150 illus. 254pp. 6⅛ x 9¼. T276 Paperbound $2.00

THE HANDBOOK OF PLANT AND FLORAL ORNAMENT,
R. G. Hatton. 1200 line illustrations, from medieval, Renaissance
herbals, of flowering or fruiting plants: garden flowers, wild
flowers, medicinal plants, poisons, industrial plants, etc. A unique
compilation that probably could not be matched in any library
in the world. Formerly "The Craftsman'sPlant-Book." Also full
text on uses, history as ornament, etc. 548pp. 6⅛ x 9¼.
T649 Paperbound $2.98

*PICTORIAL ARCHIVES: 1800 WOODCUTS FROM BEWICK
AND HIS SCHOOL.* 229 plates contain over 1800 woodcuts by
Thomas Bewick, remarkable early 19th century engraver, and
members of his school. From "Fables," "British Birds," "Quadru-
peds," and many other books and ephemera. Remarkable selec-
tion of vigorous drawings, all in line, covering nature, fashions,
activities, pastimes, arts, heraldic devices, etc. Individual items
copyright free, and may be reproduced in commercial art for
striking period effects that will catch any viewer's eye. Over
1800 illustrations. 260 pp. 9 x 12.   T766 Clothbound $10.00

VITRUVIUS: TEN BOOKS ON ARCHITECTURE. The most
influential book in the history of architecture. 1st century A.D.
Roman classic has influenced such men as Bramante, Palladio,
Michelangelo, up to present. Classic principles of design, har-
mony, etc. Fascinating reading. Definitive English translation by
Professor H. Morgan, Harvard. 344pp. 5⅜ x 8.
T645 Paperbound $2.00

*DECORATIVE ALPHABETS AND INITIALS, Alexander Nes-
bitt.* 91 complete alphabets, over 3900 ornamental initials, from
Middle Ages, Renaissance printing, baroque, rococo, and modern
sources. Individual items copyright free, for use in commercial
art, crafts, design, packaging, etc. 123 full-page plates. 3924
initials. 129pp. 7¾ x 10¾.   T544 Paperbound $2.25

*METHODS AND MATERIALS OF THE GREAT SCHOOLS
AND MASTERS, Sir Charles Eastlake.* (Formerly titled "Materials for a History of Oil Painting.") Vast, authentic reconstruc-
tion of secret techniques of the masters, recreated from ancient
manuscripts, contemporary accounts, analysis of paintings, etc.
Oils, fresco, tempera, varnishes, encaustics. Both Flemish and
Italian schools, also British and French. One of great works for
art historians, critics; inexhaustible mine of suggestions, infor-
mation for practicing artists. Total of 1025pp. 5⅜ x 8.
Two volume set, T718-9 Paperbound $4.00

*Dover publishes books on commercial art, art history, crafts, design, art
classics; also books on music, literature, science, mathematics, puzzles and
entertainments, chess, engineering, biology, philosophy, psychology, lan-
guages, history, and other fields. For free circulars write to Dept. DA,
Dover Publications, Inc., 180 Varick St., New York 14, N.Y.*